This Book Belongs To

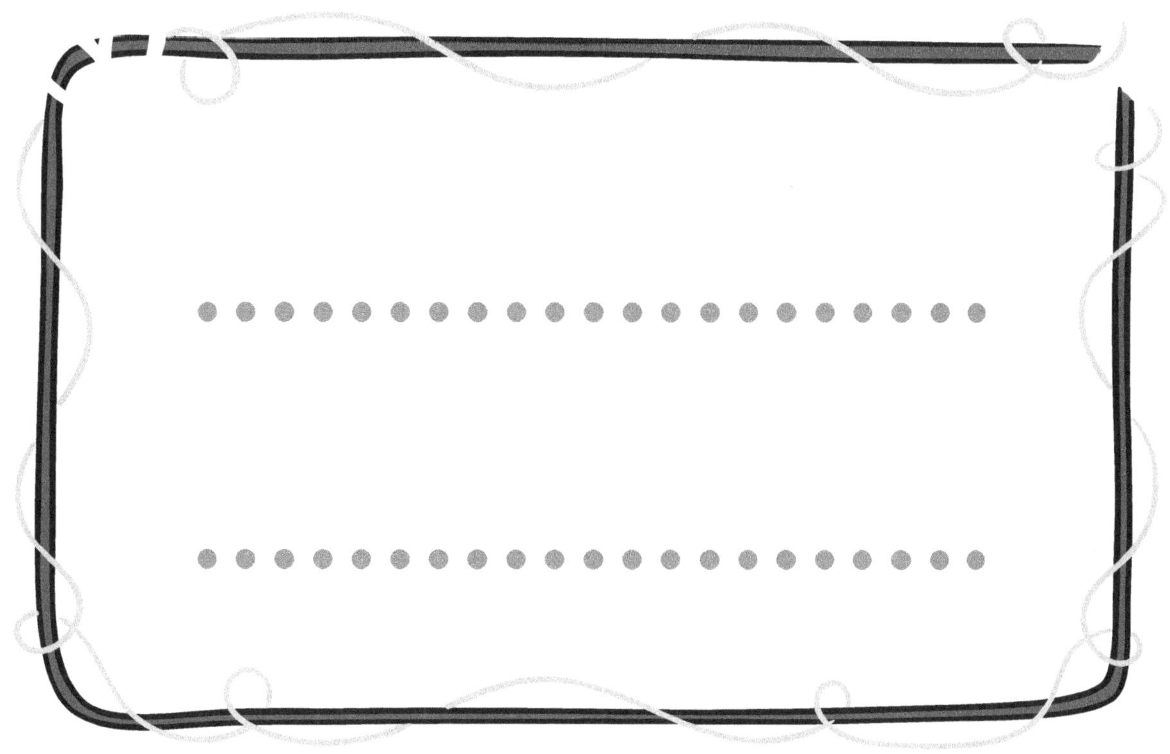

Mushroom coloring book

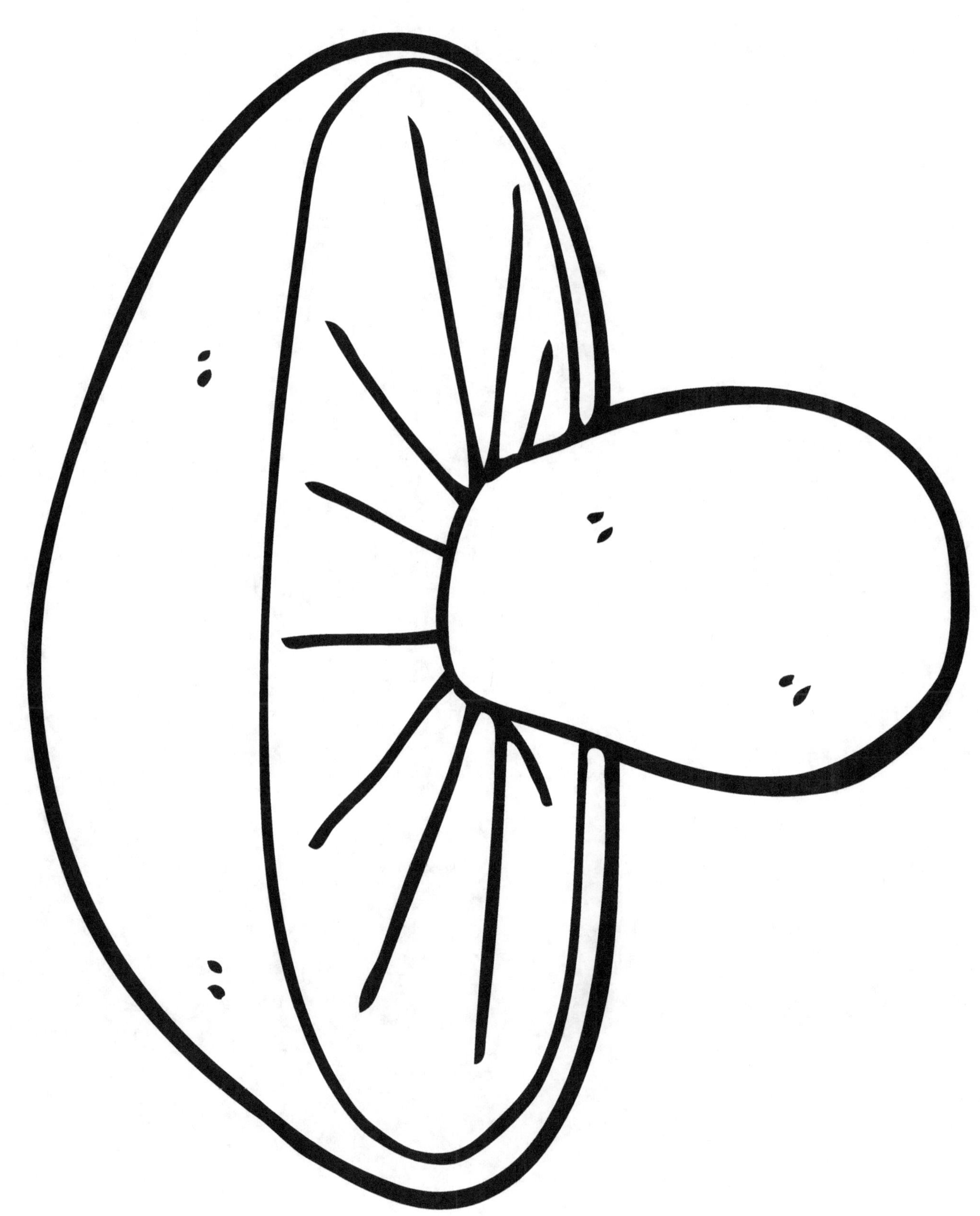

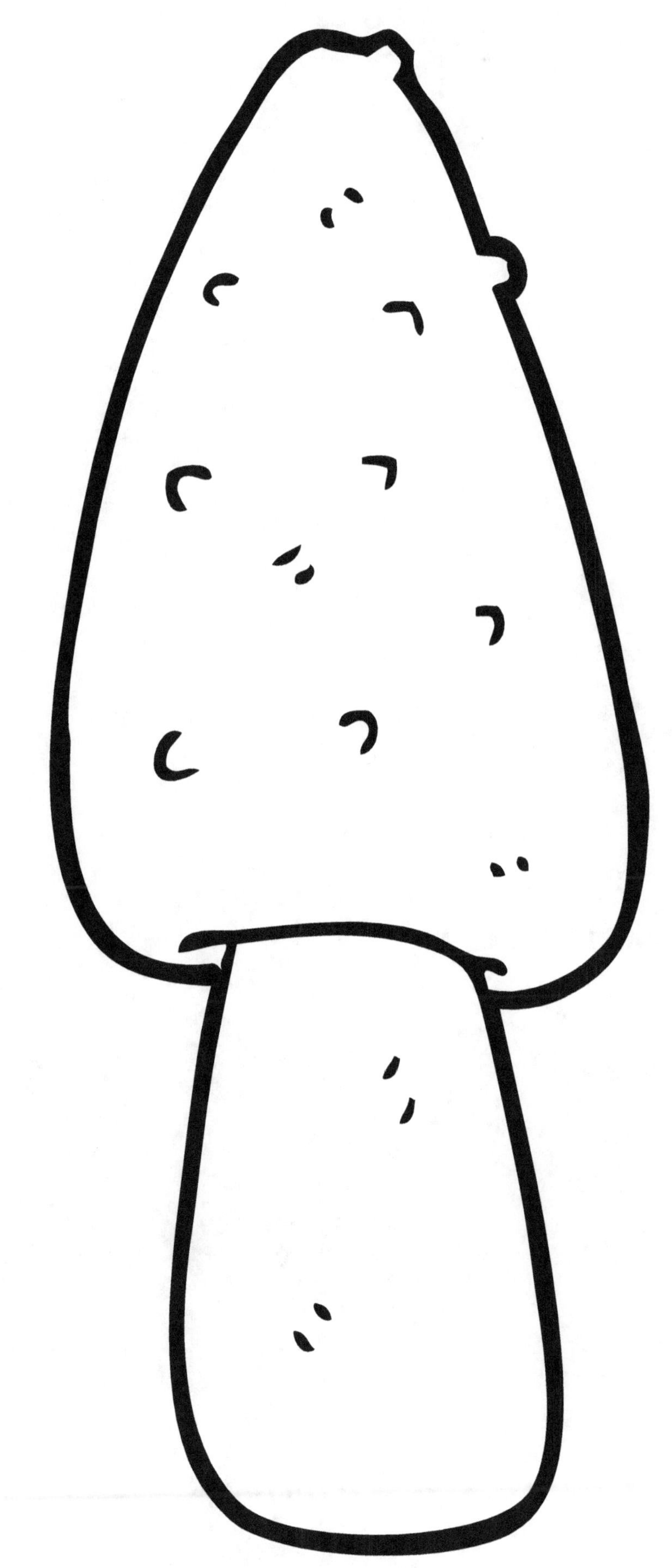

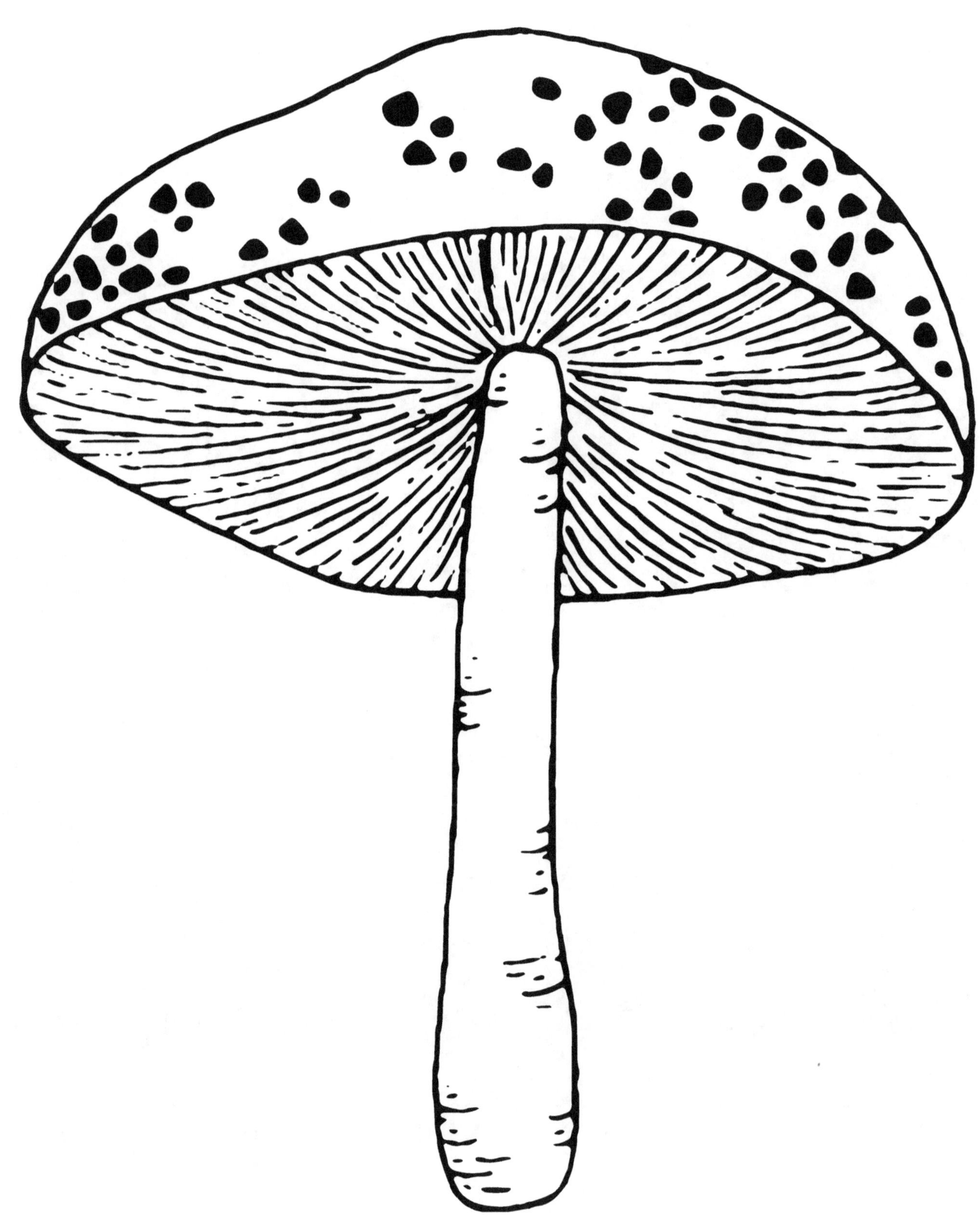

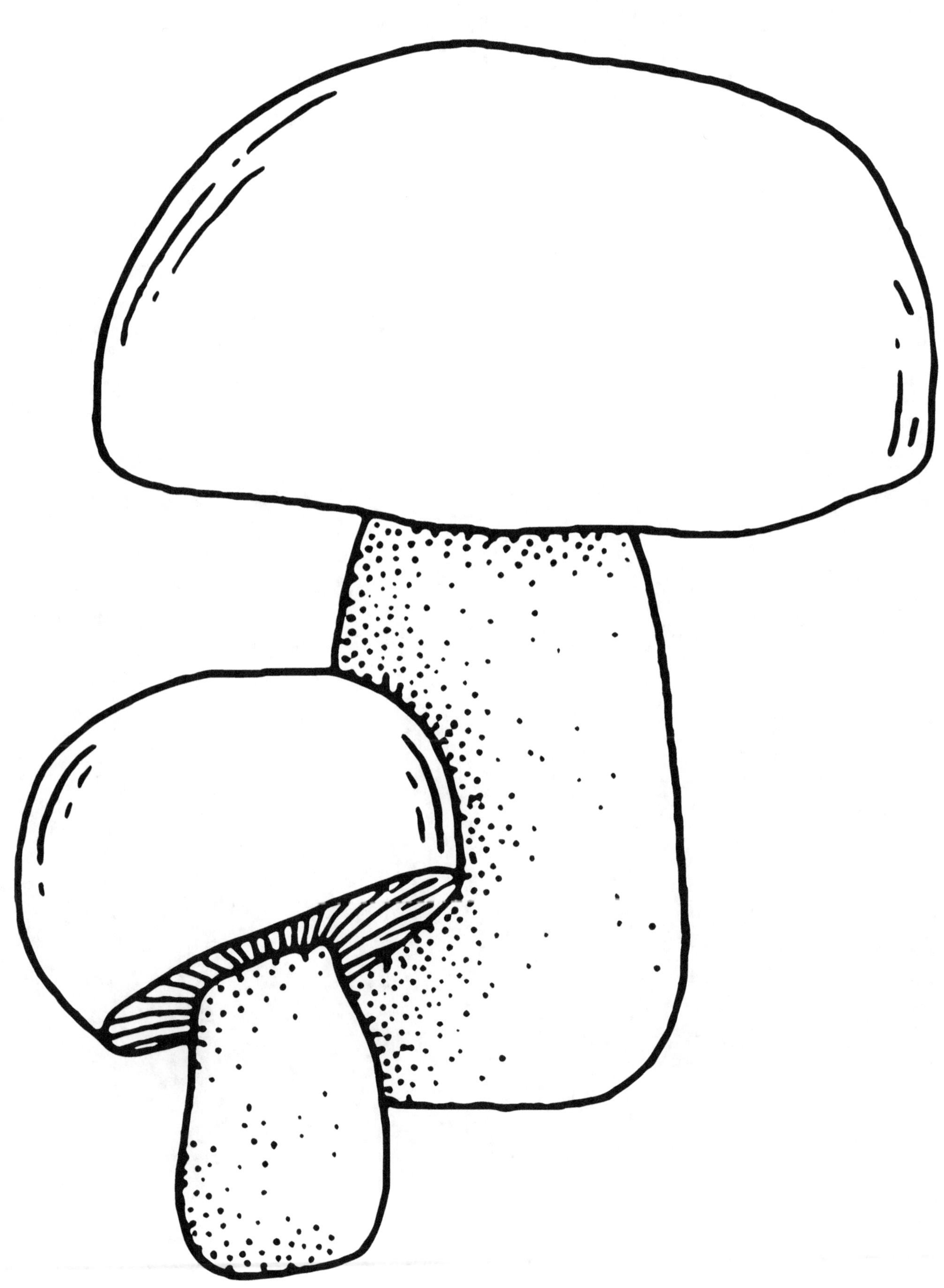

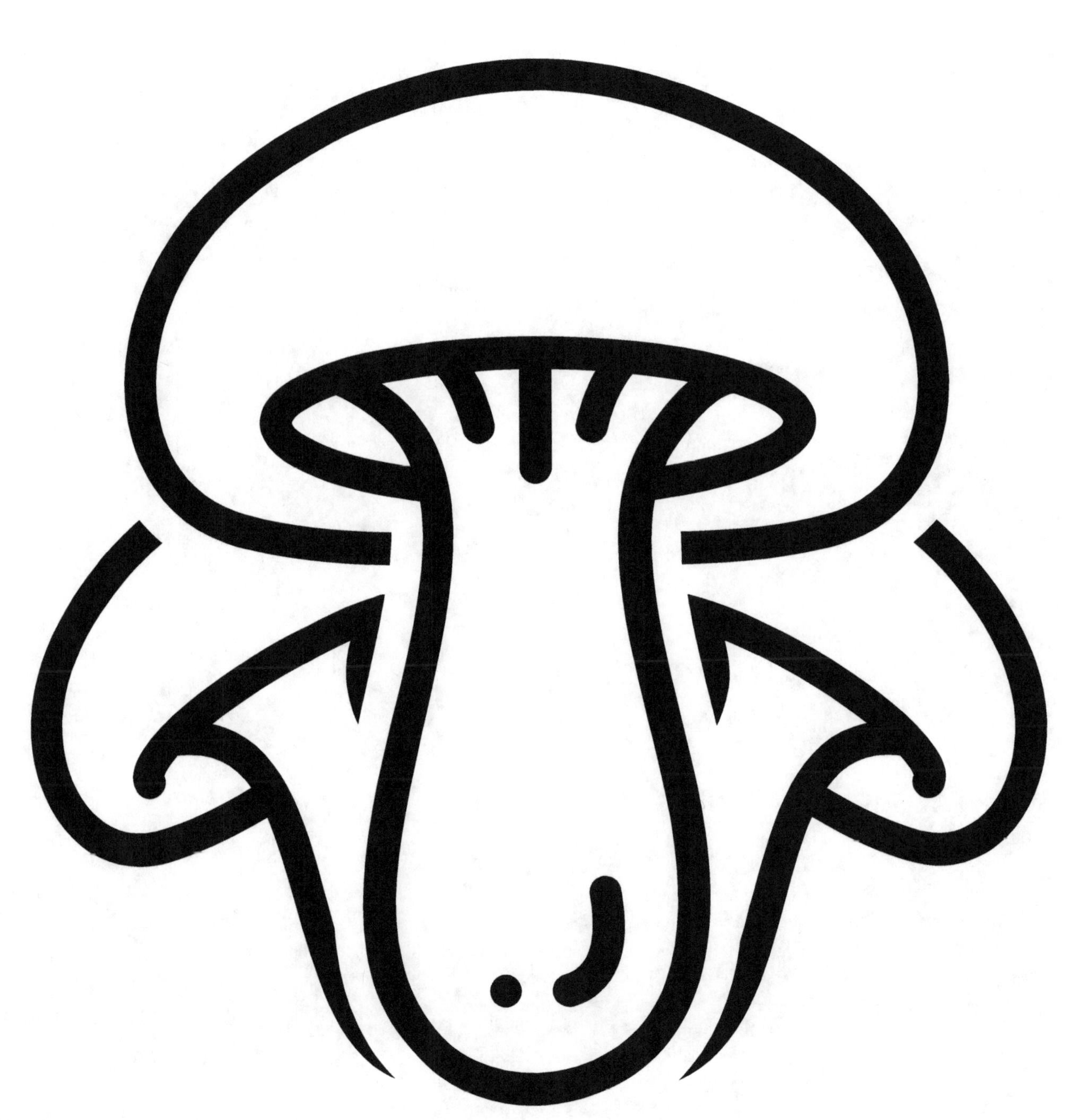

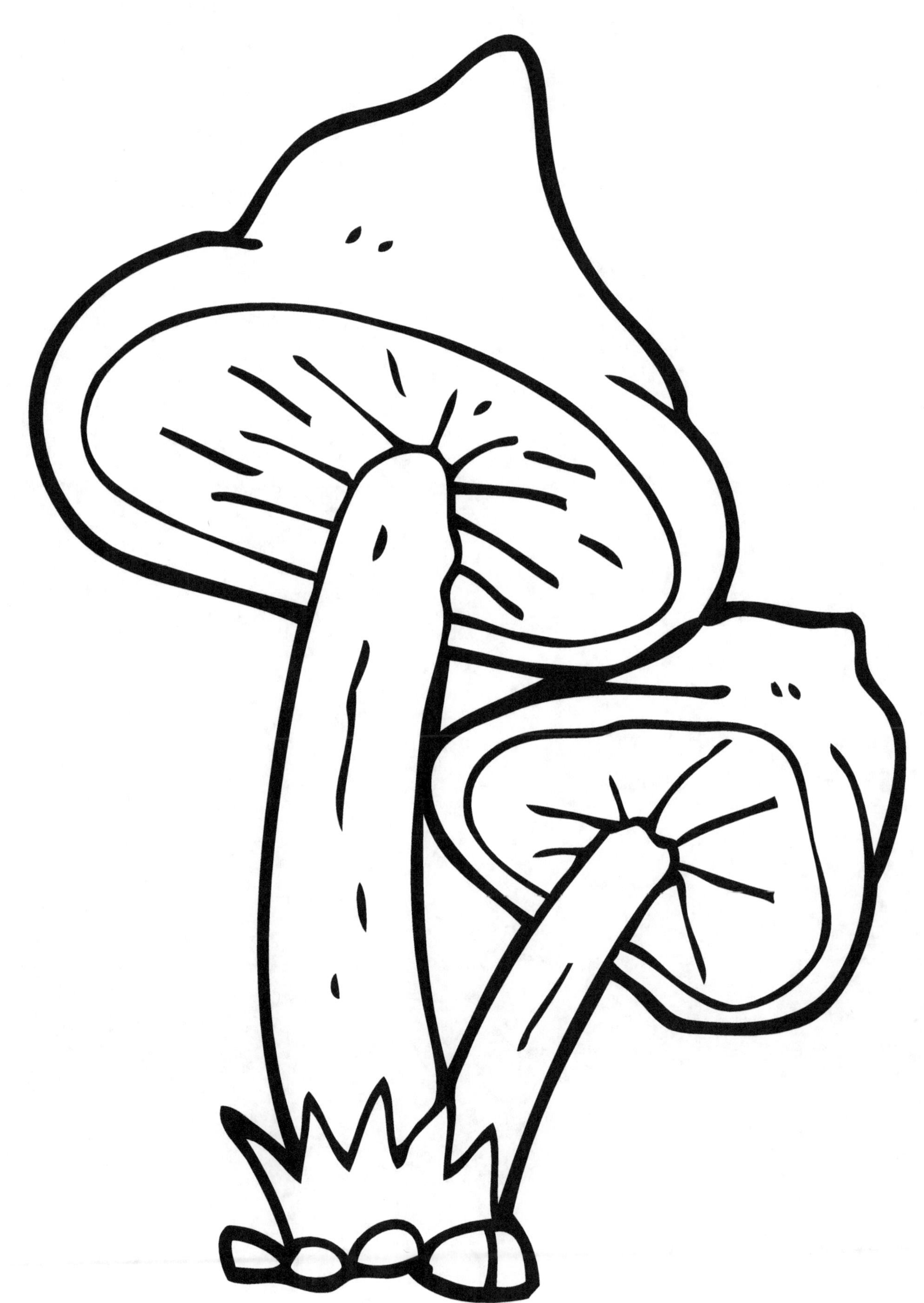

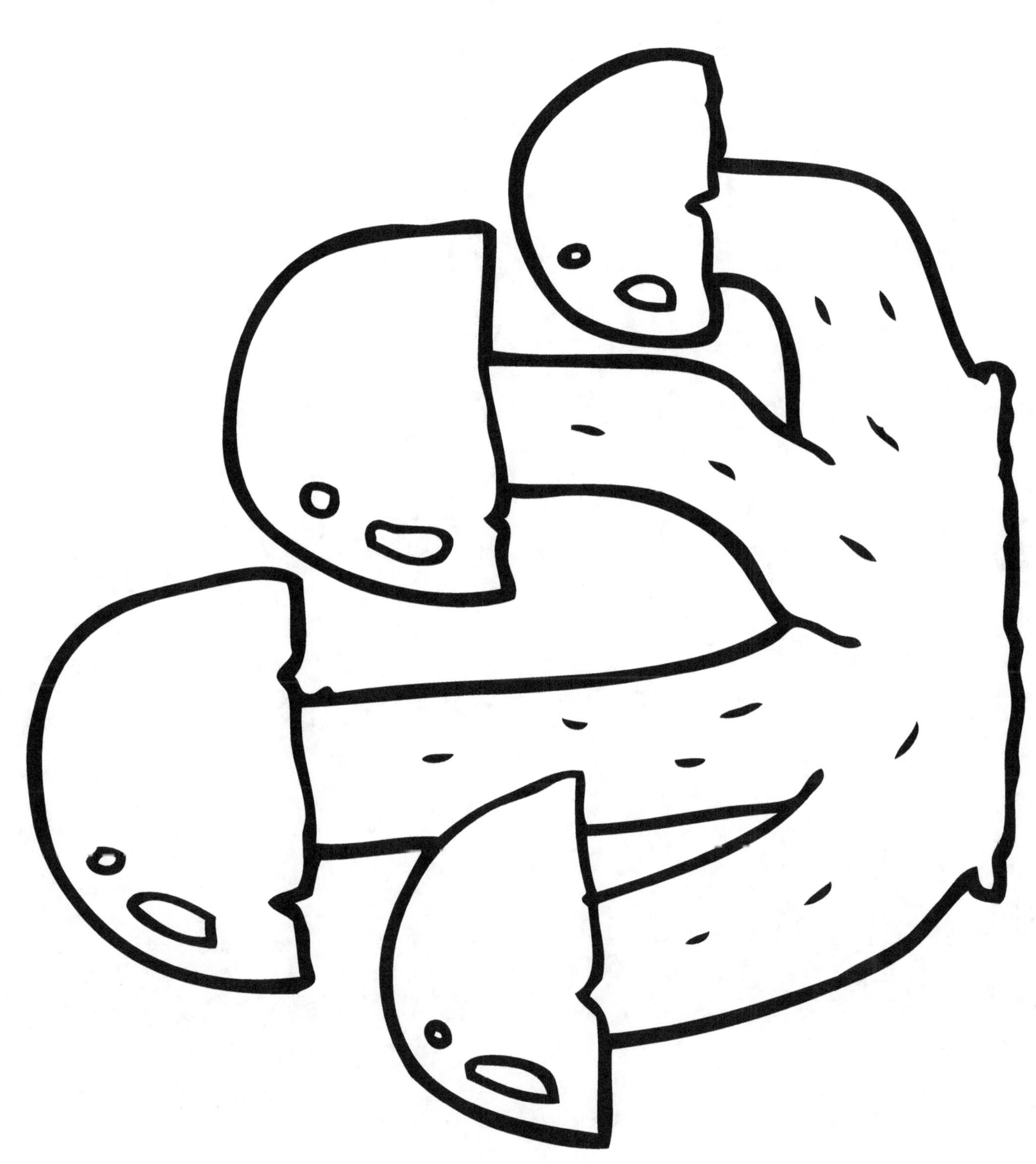

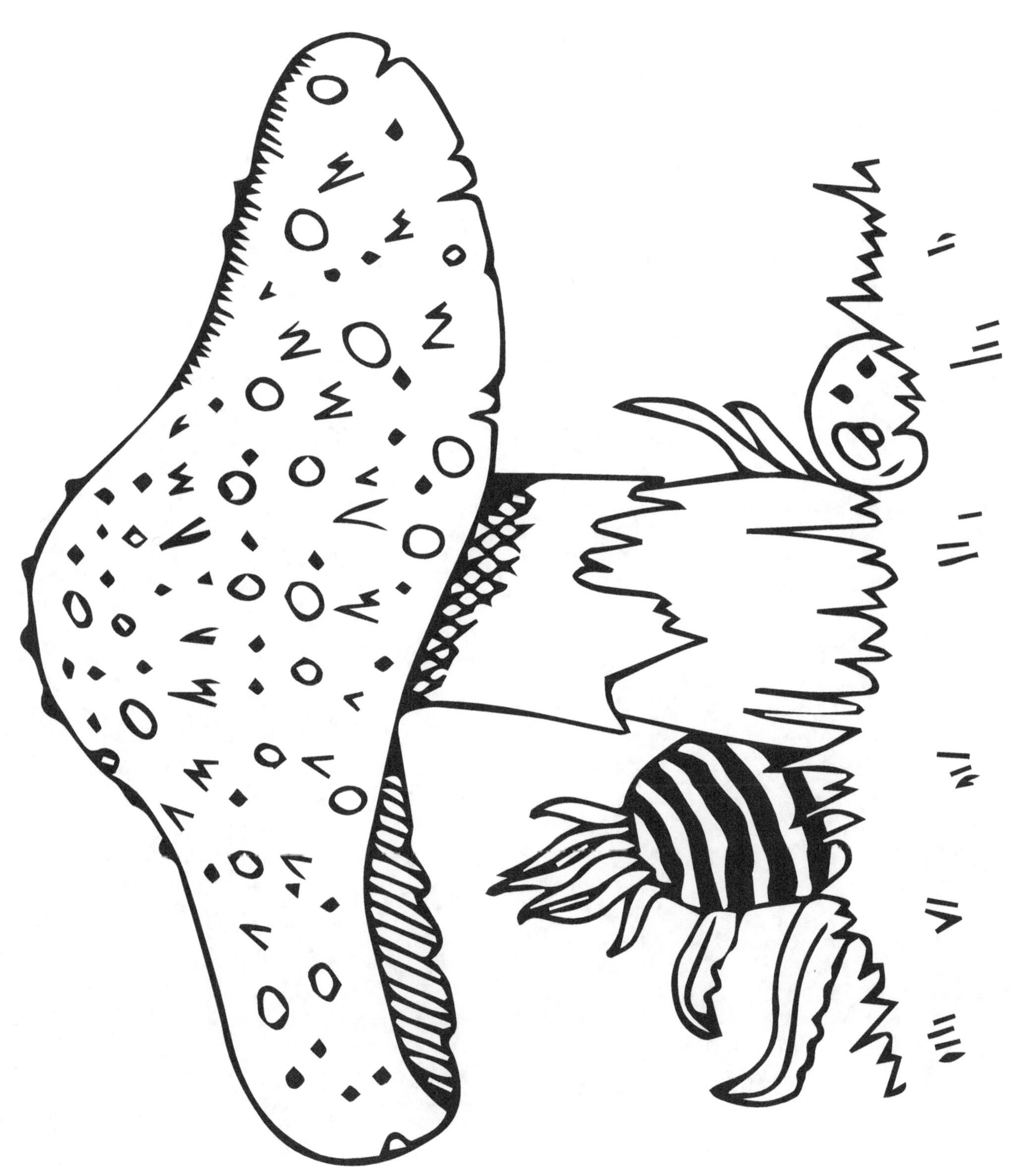

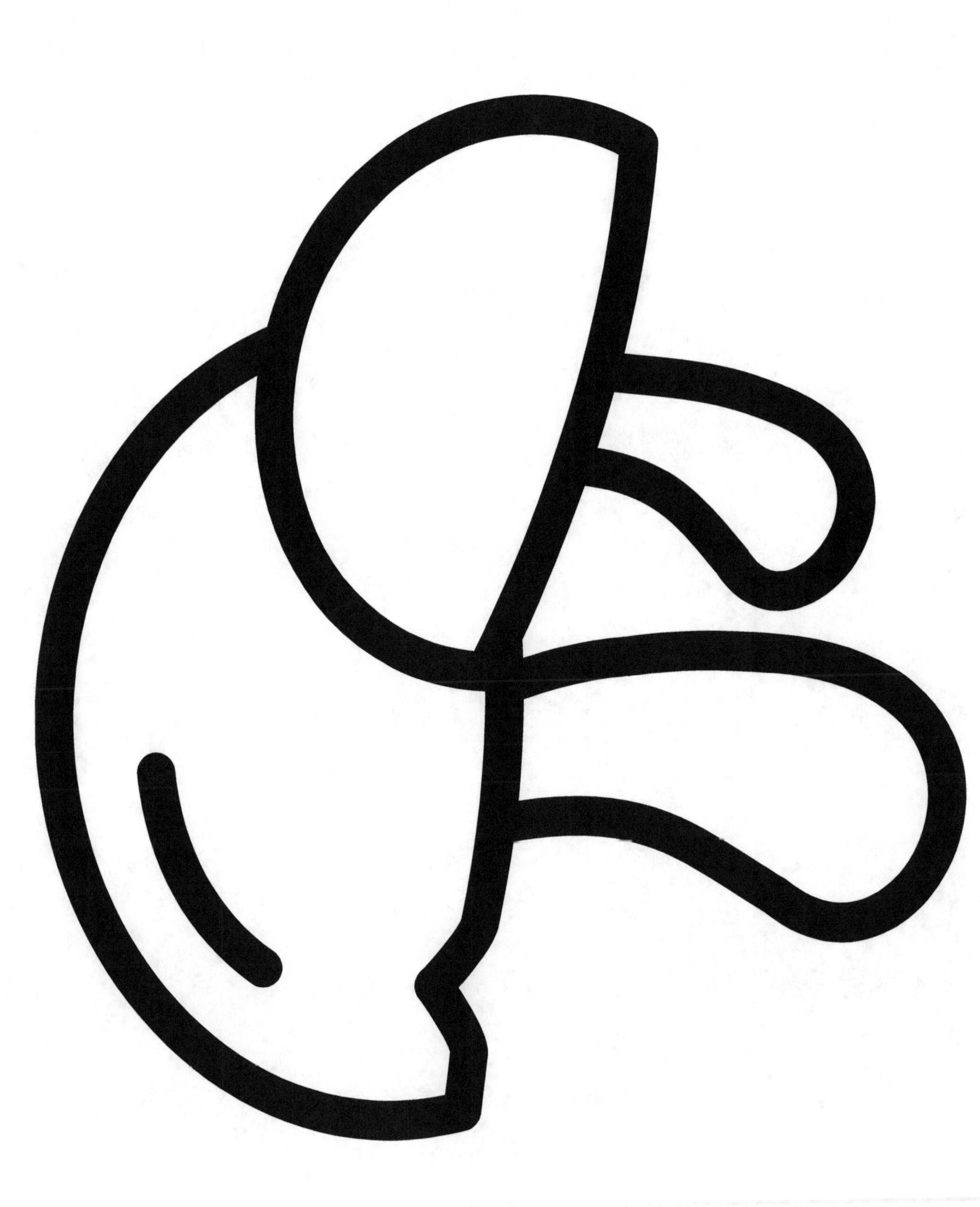

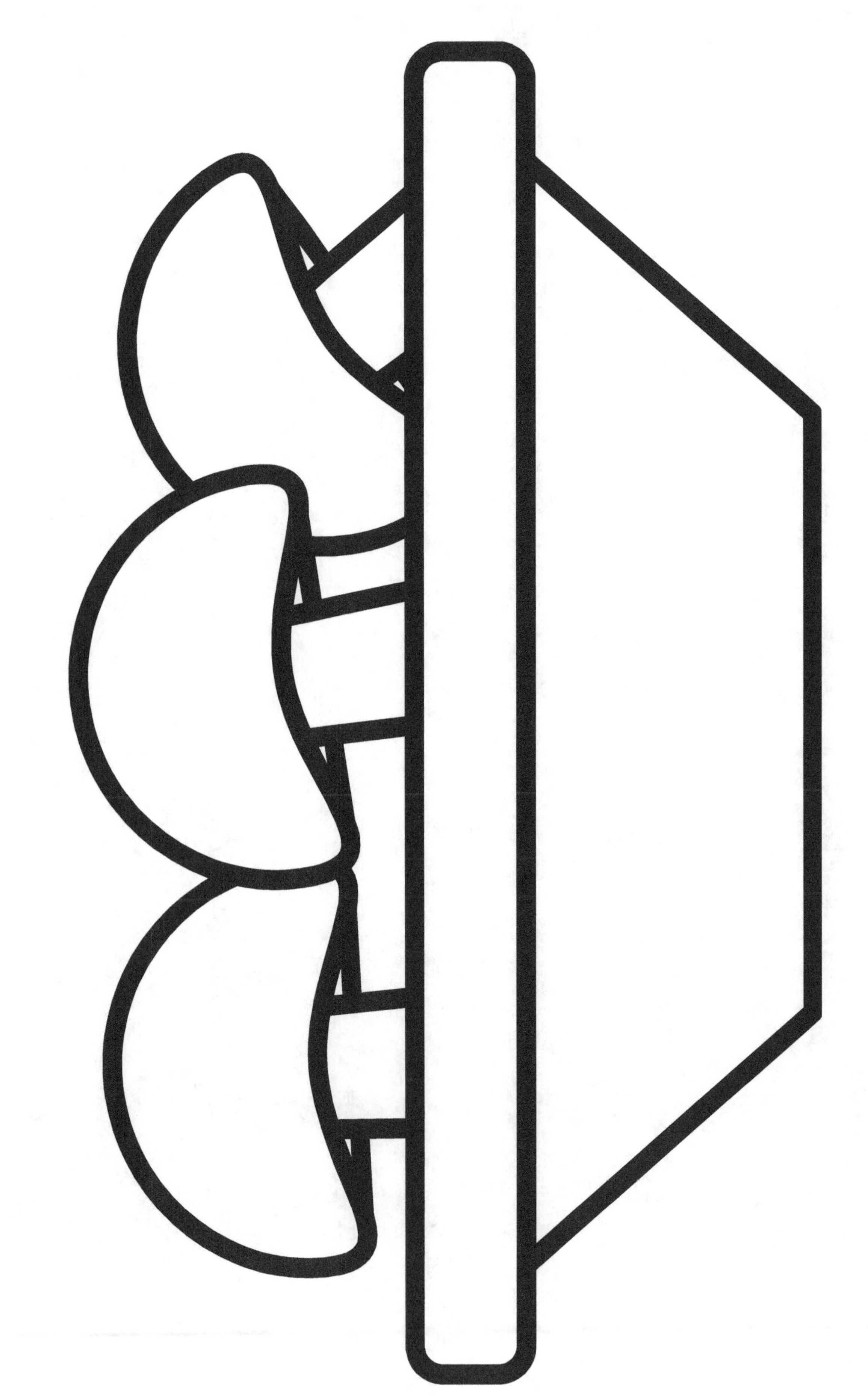

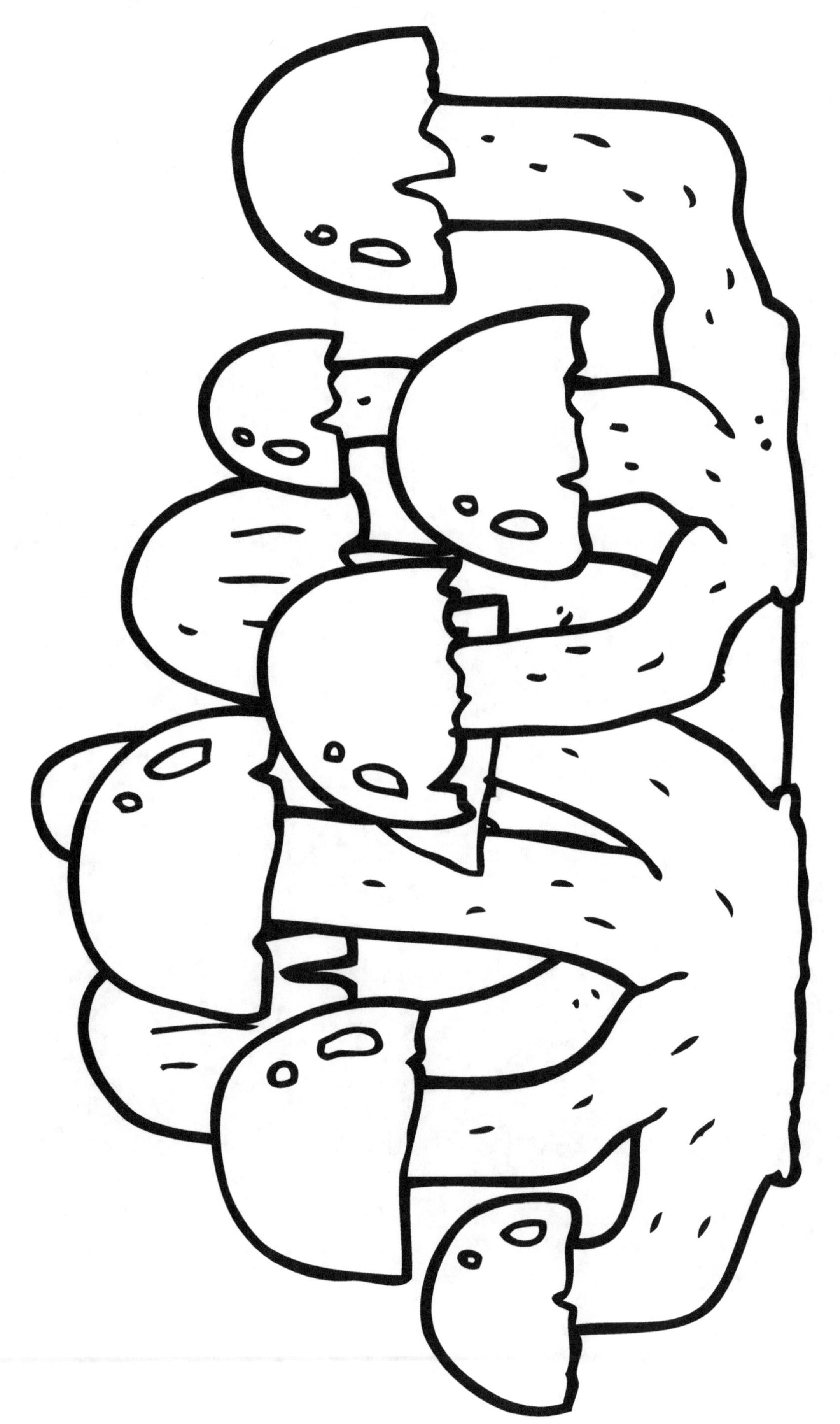

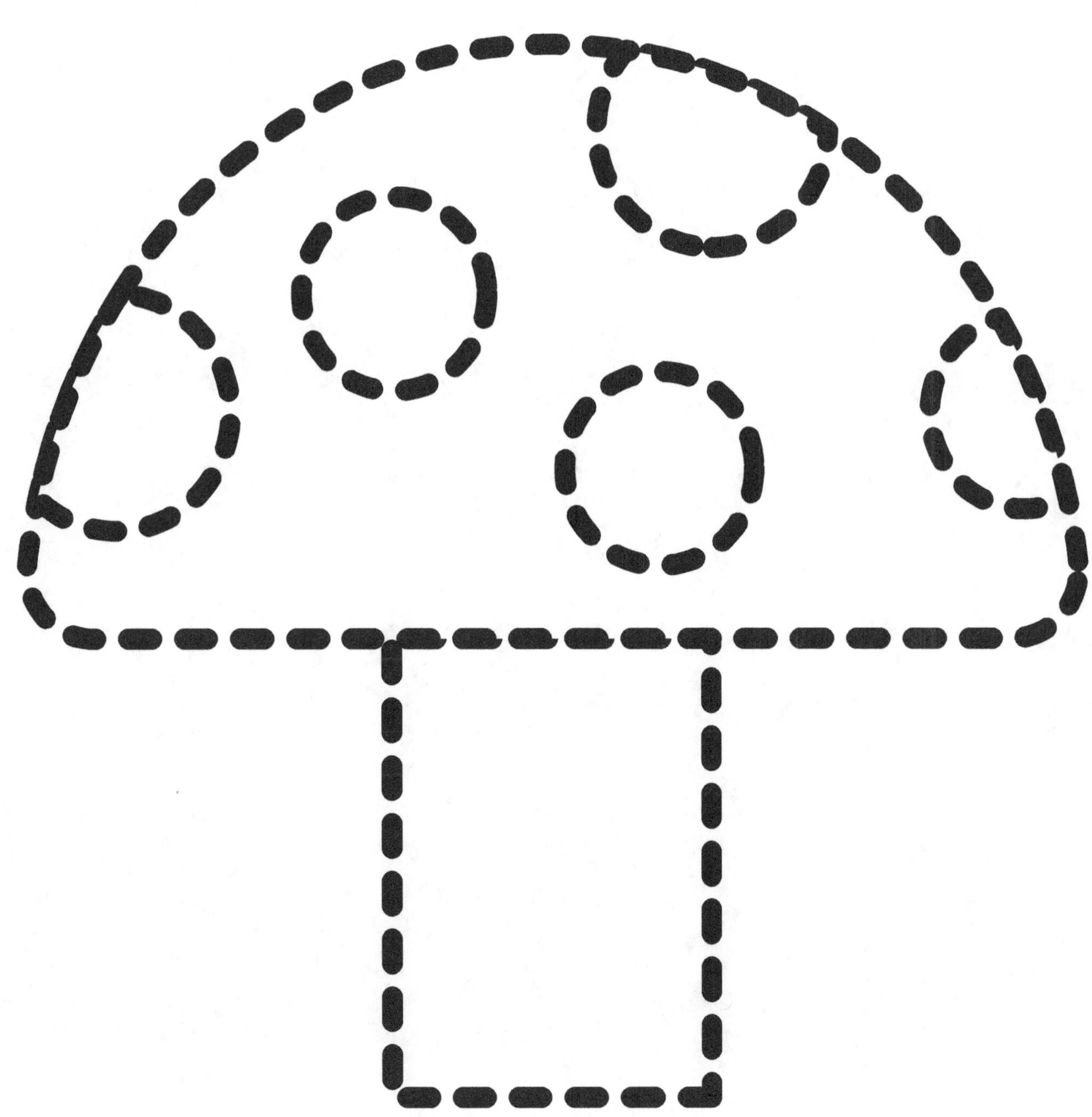